# EXPLORING ENERGY
# WOOD AND COAL

### PHILIP SAUVAIN

Editorial planning
**Deborah Tyler**

## M
### MACMILLAN

First published 1987

Published by
MACMILLAN EDUCATION LTD
Houndmills, Basingstoke, Hampshire RG21 2XS
and London
Companies and representatives
throughout the world

Designed and produced by BLA Publishing Limited,
East Grinstead, Sussex, England.

*Also in* LONDON · HONG KONG · TAIPEI · SINGAPORE · NEW YORK

**A Ling Kee Company**

Illustrations by Fiona Fordyce, Sebastian Quigley/Linden Artists, Sallie Alane Reason, Clive Spong/Linden Artists, Brian Watson/Linden Artists, Rosie Vane Wright
Colour origination by Waterden Reproductions Ltd
Printed in Hong Kong

**British Library Cataloguing in Publication Data**

Sauvain, Philip
    Exploring energy : wood and coal. —
    (Macmillan world library).
    1. Coal — Juvenile literature
    2. Fuelwood — Juvenile literature
    I. Title
    523.2'4        TN801

ISBN 0-333-44173-7
ISBN 0-333-44180-X Series

## Photographic credits

*t = top b = bottom l = left r = right*

**cover**: ZEFA, Richard Matthews/Seaphot

5, 6 ZEFA; 7*t* Panos Pictures; 7*b* Vincent Serventy/Seaphot; 8, 9*t* The Hutchison Library; 9*b* Panos Pictures; 13 National Coal Board; 14 Frank Lane Picture Agency; 15 ZEFA; 17 Mansell Collection; 19*t* ZEFA; 19*b*, 21, 22, 23*t* National Coal Board; 23 ZEFA; 26*t* Mansell Collection; 26*b* ZEFA; 27,28, National Coal Board; 31 ZEFA; 32 National Coal Board; 34 Mansell Collection; 35, 38, 41 ZEFA; 42 Richard Matthews/Seaphot; 43*t*, 43*b* National Coal Board; 45 Anthony Joyce/Seaphot

**Note to the reader**
In this book there are some words in the text which are printed in **bold** type. This shows that the word is listed in the glossary on page 46. The glossary gives a brief explanation of words which may be new to you.

# Contents

# Introduction

We give the name **work** to any kind of action or movement. Machines work, so do people. We need energy to do work. Energy makes things move. It gives us heat and light. It helps plants grow. All the energy used on Earth comes from the Sun. You cannot see this energy. You cannot make it or destroy it. It always changes into something else when it is used.

## Food

All living things use energy. They get that energy from food. You get your energy when you eat plants or when you eat meat. You use up this energy when you walk, run, swim and even when you sleep. This is why you feel hungry after a ball game, like football, and when you wake up. Your body wants new energy from food.

We count the energy in food in **calories**. The number of calories you use depends on how fast you move. You use up more calories when you run than when you sit.

There are other types of energy. Heat energy from the Sun helps plants to grow. They store that energy in the part of the plant we use as food. When we eat this food, the stored energy, which once came from the Sun, passes from the plants to us. When our muscles move, we use this stored energy. We turn it back into heat and energy once more. All these changes make up the **energy cycle**.

**Uses of energy throughout the world**

coal

oil

natural gas

wood and plants

other sources of energy e.g. nuclear energy

Sun

water

water

Earth's heat

wind

## Machines and energy

Until about 8000 years ago, the only energy people had came from their muscles. Then, they began to use animals. Later, they used wind and moving water to turn wheels.

Machines, like cars and washing machines, make life easier for us. Energy makes the machines work. Most machines get their energy from **fuel**. Fuel comes from the Sun in much the same way that we get food. About 300 million years ago, growing trees, plants and creatures stored heat and light from the Sun. After they died, the remains were buried under mud and sand. Over millions of years, the remains were squeezed until they turned into fuel, like coal and oil. These fuels are used by machines to turn the stored energy from the Sun back into heat or work.

A lot of the world's fuel has been used up already. This is because wood can be replaced, but coal or oil cannot. People will have to find new energy in the future to make their machines work.

▼ Digging coal out of a hillside is hard work. This huge machine can do much more work than a person. It does not get tired, but it uses a lot of fuel.

# Wood as a fuel

Heat and light from the Sun make trees grow. Trees store this energy from the Sun as wood. The stored energy turns back into heat and light when you burn the wood on a fire. Most people used wood as a fuel until 200 years ago. Trees were more common than grass in the past, and they once covered two-thirds of the world. Trees cover only a quarter of the world today. They were cut down to make more land for farming.

## How wood burns

Fires burn because they use a gas called **oxygen** from the air. This is why a puff of air can make a dying fire blaze up again. Wood burns quickly because it contains a lot of oxygen. Wood also contains a lot of a substance called **carbon** and a small amount of a gas called **hydrogen**. All plants contain carbon, oxygen and hydrogen.

Wood will still burn slowly if it is covered to keep air from getting to the fire. This is because of the amount of oxygen in the wood. The wood gives off gases in the form of smoke and turns into black **charcoal**. Charcoal can also be used as a fuel. It has twice the amount of energy as wood because it is almost all carbon.

◀ **This man earns his living by making charcoal in the forests of West Germany. He collects the wood and carefully makes the stack. It will be several days before the wood turns into charcoal. While the wood smokes in the background, he uses the flames of a wood fire to cook his food.**

## Buying and using wood

People in many parts of the world still use wood fires for all their cooking and heating. Dead wood found lying on the ground is usually free. In countries where there are few trees there is not much wood. People in many African towns have to buy the wood for their fires at a market.

Big firms own most of the forests in Europe and the United States. Wood from these trees is used to make furniture or paper. It is not used as fuel. Many people think it is wasteful to burn wood on a fire.

## Disappearing forests

There should be plenty of wood in the world. Trees are easy to plant. This is why wood is called a **renewable** fuel. Instead, many of the world's trees have been cut down to make way for crops, roads and towns. When forests are cut down and no new trees are planted, this is called **deforestation**. The world's forests will disappear if new trees are not planted soon to take their place. We need to plant two new trees for each old tree we cut down.

▲ These people are buying fuel wood at a market in India. The wood is being weighed. People who have to buy wood use it carefully. They do not waste it.

▼ The woodlands of the world get smaller every minute. Chopping down the trees has turned this part of Tasmania into a wasteland.

# Wood for cooking

People used wood fires to cook meat over 100 000 years ago. Cooking makes meat tender instead of tough and hard to chew. Children and old people find it easier to eat cooked meat than raw meat. Many people still use wood fires for cooking food. Children at a summer camp like to cook a meal over a wood fire. Some people like to cook with wood as their fuel all the time. They use special **stoves** which burn wood.

## Collecting wood

Many people in Africa and Asia have to cook over a wood fire. There are few other fuels they can use for cooking. They look for dead wood which is dry. They use small twigs to start a fire and larger logs to make it burn slowly. They choose woods which give off less smoke than others.

They know which woods are best to collect if they want the fire to burn quickly. They know which woods stay hot for a long time.

Women and children often have the job of looking for wood. In some parts of Africa, there are so few trees that women have to walk five kilometres a day carrying heavy loads of wood on their heads. They put the fire out as soon as their meal is cooked to save fuel.

## Cooking over an open fire

Three stones placed in a fire are all that is needed to cook food over a wood fire. The pot of food rests on the three stones so it is above the hottest ashes in the middle of the fire. Fires like this can be seen in many countries, such as Niger in Africa and Fiji in the Pacific Ocean. In these hot countries, people like to cook outside, in the shade.

▼ **Would you like to have to look for wood every day? This is the job many children have to do in places where there are no other fuels.**

## Using stoves

Cooking over an open fire outside wastes the energy in the wood. Most of the heat goes up into the air and is lost forever. Rain and wind make it hard to keep the fire alight. Gusts of wind can quickly spread the flames from a fire to a tent or a house. This is why so many people in India use wood-burning stoves to cook on instead of open fires. The stove keeps the heat inside, so it makes better use of the heat. It also saves fuel. The best stoves use charcoal which burns more slowly and gives off more heat.

◄ Cooking food over a wood fire is not always easy. The wind can blow the fire out. The wind can also make the fire flare up and make it too hot.

▼ This woman is cooking on a stove built of bricks. The bricks keep in the heat. She is using wood and charcoal as fuel.

# The first forests

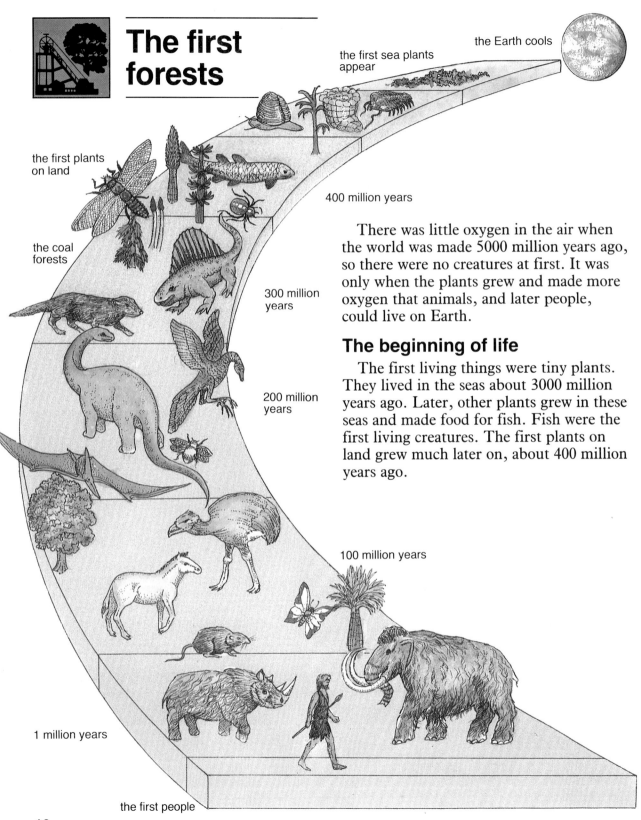

the Earth cools

the first sea plants appear

400 million years

the first plants on land

the coal forests

300 million years

200 million years

100 million years

1 million years

the first people

There was little oxygen in the air when the world was made 5000 million years ago, so there were no creatures at first. It was only when the plants grew and made more oxygen that animals, and later people, could live on Earth.

## The beginning of life

The first living things were tiny plants. They lived in the seas about 3000 million years ago. Later, other plants grew in these seas and made food for fish. Fish were the first living creatures. The first plants on land grew much later on, about 400 million years ago.

## The coal forests

A lot of oxygen was made about 300 million years ago. This was a time when very hot, wet weather helped thick forests and huge ferns to grow. The ground was swampy and covered in a thick mat of rotting leaves. This was long before there were people on Earth.

The forests grew well for 80 million years. This length of time is called the **Carboniferous period** because plants made a lot of carbon then. Much of this carbon later turned into coal. This is why the millions of trees which grew in the Carboniferous period are sometimes called the coal forests.

## The Sun, plants and people

The first people lived on Earth about one million years ago. People live by breathing in oxygen from the air. We breathe out a gas called **carbon dioxide** which we do not need. Trees and plants make the oxygen we need. Their leaves hold a green substance called **chlorophyll**. It uses sunlight to turn the carbon dioxide in the air into carbon and oxygen. The plant uses the carbon to make its food. It does this by mixing the carbon with water which it gets from the soil through its roots. The plant releases the unwanted oxygen.

▼ The trees and plants in this forest grew 300 million years ago. Their remains turned into the rock we call coal.

# Hidden fuels

## How rocks and fossils are formed

1. Millions of years ago, dead trees and plants lay in the shallow seas that covered a lot of the Earth.

2. Year after year, rivers washed bits of rock, mud and sand down to the sea. They sank to the seabed.

3. The weight of so many layers of sediment slowly turned them into rocks. Dead plants and animals were squashed between the layers.

Millions of years ago, rivers cut away stones, mud and sand from the side of the valleys they flowed through. The stones, mud and sand were carried by the rivers to the sea. There they settled on the seabed.

The layers of mud and sand sometimes covered the remains of dead creatures and kept them from rotting away completely. The weight, or **pressure**, of the new layers of mud and sand slowly turned the remains into stone. Plants or creatures preserved in stone are called **fossils**.

## Rocks and fossils

Each new layer of mud and sand, or **sediment**, lay flat and pressed down on the layers below. The pressure made the sediment solid. Over millions of years it turned into a hard rock called **sedimentary rock**. Fossils are found only in sedimentary rock.

---

▶ Sometimes, miners find plant fossils on a piece of coal. This fern reminds us that coal was once a tree which grew in a forest with ferns.

## Fossil fuels

Coal and oil are called **fossil fuels**. This is because, like fossils, the remains of great piles of dead trees and plants were buried under layers of sediment. The remains of trees and plants changed slowly under pressure into coal. The remains of many tiny sea creatures changed into oil. When we burn coal or oil today, we make use of the Sun's energy from the time of the coal forests.

4. When parts of the Earth moved, some of the rocks came to the surface and became dry land.

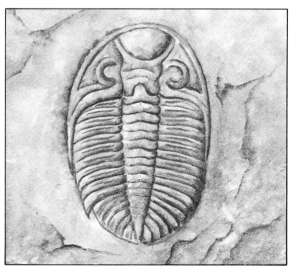

5. Fossils of plants and animals are sometimes found in these sedimentary rocks.

# What is coal?

Sometimes, we can tell that coal once started life as wood. Some lumps of coal have the same markings as wood. People have found perfect fossils in coal, such as the prints of a leaf or fern. The prints are often found between thin layers in the coal. These fossils are from the time of the coal forests about 300 million years ago.

## How coal was made

The tree and plant remains of the coal forests slowly changed. They changed into a type of soft coal, called **peat**, then into brown coal, then finally into black coal. The more pressure there was on the tree and plant remains, the harder and blacker the coal became.

Coal is made up mostly of carbon, with some oxygen and some hydrogen. Coal is found all over the world in layers called **seams**. Most of these coal seams lie deep below the ground. This is because coal can only be made under a great weight of rocks. The coal seams are near the surface in some places because of earth movements after the seams were made. Sometimes, the coal seam can be seen on the surface because the rocks above it have been washed away by rivers.

## Types of coal

Different types of coal have different amounts of carbon in them. Coal formed at the greatest depths has the most carbon. This is because it has been under the greatest pressure. The coal with the most carbon gives off the most heat. It is also hardest to light because it has less gas in it. Coal formed nearer to the surface has the least carbon because it has been under the least pressure.

▼ A seam of coal can be seen on the side of the valley where the Healy River in Alaska has cut through the rocks.

**Types of coal**

▲ Peat is found near the surface in wet ground. It is cut with a special spade. Then it is piled up and dried. After a few months, it can be burned in a fire.

Peat is coal in the making. It is made from partly rotted plants which are found in soft boggy ground. Peat shows us what today's coal looked like millions of years ago. Peat is soft and spongy to touch, but it can be dried out and used as a fuel. **Lignite** is a brown coal which crumbles easily and looks woody. Lignite is a young coal as there is very little sediment above it to make it hard and black. Lignite is often found close to the surface. It is easier to mine than other coals. It does not give off much heat. **Cannel coal** is a harder coal, but it still breaks easily. It burns slowly with a flame like a candle. **Bituminous coal**, or house coal, is the softest and most easily broken of the hard coals. It gives off gases when it is burned. This is why you can see yellow flames and smoke in a coal fire. **Anthracite** has the most carbon. This is the oldest and hardest type of coal. It is smokeless and burns very slowly.

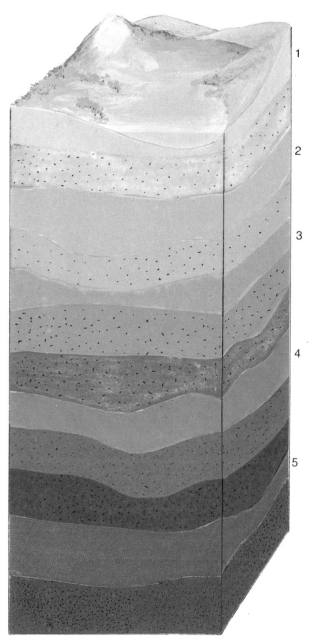

1 peat

2 lignite

3 cannel coal

4 bituminous coal

5 anthracite

# The first coal mines

▼ Coal was brought up from bell pits in buckets. Horses walking around and around were often used to wind the buckets up. Sometimes, a bucket of coal overturned as it got to the top of the pit. Falls of rock were common in the mine, too. The falls made mining dangerous work.

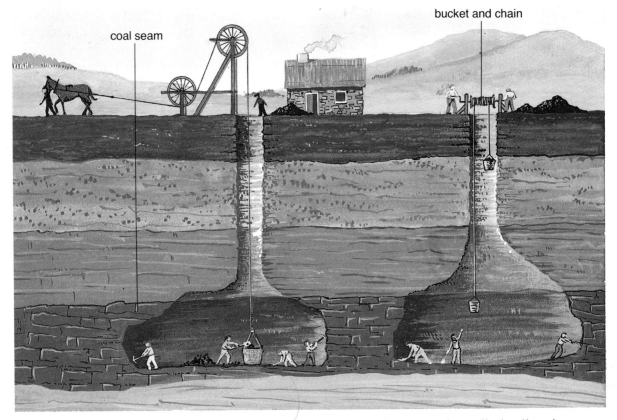

coal seam

bucket and chain

Coal has been used as a fuel for hundreds of years. Roman soldiers used it in some parts of Europe 2000 years ago. The Italian explorer, Marco Polo, saw people burning 'black stones' in China in about 1275. Most people used wood as their main fuel because there were plenty of forests. As the forests were cut down, people had to find other fuels.

## Digging for coal

At first, people found coal washed up on a beach or in coal seams in a hillside. This coal was easy to find. When it was used up, miners had to get at the coal below the ground.

Some dug tunnels, called **adit mines**, into the coal seams on the sides of hills. They dug out the coal until the roof fell in. Other miners dug down into **bell pits** for their coal. They dug a hole, or **shaft**, three to six metres deep. Then they cut out the coal around the bottom of the shaft, so that the shaft looked like a bell. The first coal miners soon found that coal mining was dangerous. Tunnels fell in with the weight of the rocks above. The miners needed to find a safer way of digging for coal. One good idea was to leave half the coal standing as pillars of rock to hold up the tunnels. This is called **room and pillar** mining.

Miners sometimes used another way of mining in order to mine more coal. They used the **longwall** method. Many miners worked together to take the coal from the whole length, or long wall, of the coal seam at the same time. They built stone walls and used timber posts, or **props**, to hold up the roof.

## Dangers

Deep pits made mining more dangerous. Tunnels filled with water from underground streams, and miners drowned. The old way of using people to take the water away in a long chain of buckets did not work against floods. This is why, in about 1700, the first steam engines were used to pump water out of the mines. The steam engines could pump the water all the time, so the miners could dig deeper. Explosions killed many miners when candle flames or sparks set fire to **methane gas** trapped inside a coal seam. There were other gases which choked the miners when they breathed them in. In 1815, Humphrey Davy invented the **safety lamp**. It meant that for the first time miners could carry a light safely into the mines. The lamp also helped to save lives. The flame changed colour if the dangerous methane gas was in the mine. Coal mining today is much safer than it was in the past, but each year many miners are killed or hurt in accidents in mines all over the world.

▼ This is a room and pillar mine about 200 years ago. The miners are working by candlelight. Good coal is wasted in the pillars which support the roof.

# Coal near the surface

In some countries, there are coal seams close to the surface. This coal is easier and not so dangerous to mine. Nearly half the coal mined in the United States and in New South Wales, Australia, comes from surface mining. One seam of lignite in Australia is 250 metres thick.

## Surface mining

Mining coal from near the surface is called **opencast** or **strip mining**. The miners strip away the earth on top of the coal so they can mine it more easily.

Strip mining begins when diggers and shovels are used to remove the earth to get at the coal below. They may have to move 30 tonnes of soil and rock to get at each tonne of coal. The best soil on top, the **topsoil**, is put in one pile. The other earth, the **overburden**, is put in a second pile.

This makes it easier to put the topsoil back on top after the coal has been mined.

Large diggers take the coal out of the ground. Their huge buckets hold several hundred tonnes of coal at a time. The coal is loaded straight on to huge trucks or on to **conveyor belts**, which take the coal to the trucks.

Strip mining begins when diggers and shovels are used to remove the earth to get at the coal below. They may have to move 30 tonnes of soil and rock to get at each tonne of coal. The best soil on top, the **topsoil**, is put in one pile. The other earth, the **overburden**, is put in a second pile.

Strip mining has some disadvantages, too. The big diggers are noisy when they are in use and they are costly to buy. Strip mines are ugly and spoil the look of the land. Many American strip mines have just been left as ugly holes in the ground. This causes a lot of anger. Local people try to make mining companies fill in the strips, plant trees and sow grass. Even when they do, the fields and woodland take many years to grow again.

**A strip mine**

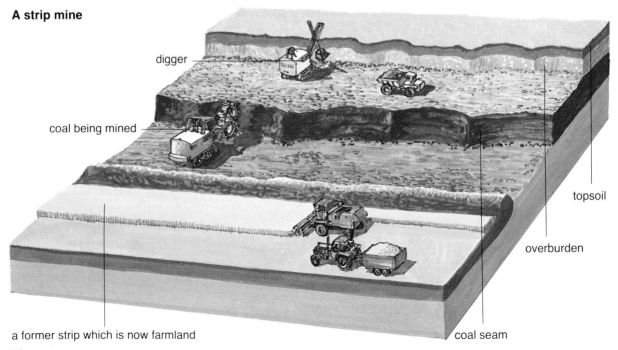

digger

coal being mined

topsoil

overburden

a former strip which is now farmland

coal seam

▲ Huge machines dig out coal from an opencast mine at Frechen in West Germany. The machine in the middle is a bucket wheel excavator. It can dig about 2000 tonnes of coal a day.

▶ The tunnels of the Betws drift mine in Wales leave the green countryside above unspoiled. The coal comes to the surface by the conveyor belt on the right.

## Sloping mines

Some coal mines are called **drift mines**. These are mines where the coal is near the surface, but it is too deep for strip mining. Drift miners dig a long sloping tunnel to reach the coal. Then, conveyor belts bring the coal straight up to the surface.

# Searching for coal

The number of people in the world, or the world's **population**, grows bigger all the time. People want more energy each year for heating and cooking. Machines need more power. These demands for more energy are met by burning more coal to make **electricity**. Coal is a **non-renewable** fuel. It cannot be renewed by planting trees. Once coal is used, it has gone for ever. This is why people look for new seams of coal. They hope to find coal which will be easy to mine and to move.

## Surveys

**Geologists** are people who study the rocks. They look for places where they think coal may be found. Then, they drill rows of small holes in the ground. A series of small explosions is set off. The geologists take measurements as the noise travels through the rocks. This is called a **seismic survey**. They can tell from the results of the survey if there are likely to be coal seams below the ground.

Next, they find out about the rocks under the ground by looking at samples of rock. A sample is taken out of the ground with a test drill. The machine drills a **borehole** deep into the ground and takes out a long strip of earth and rock, called a core. The geologists can measure the width

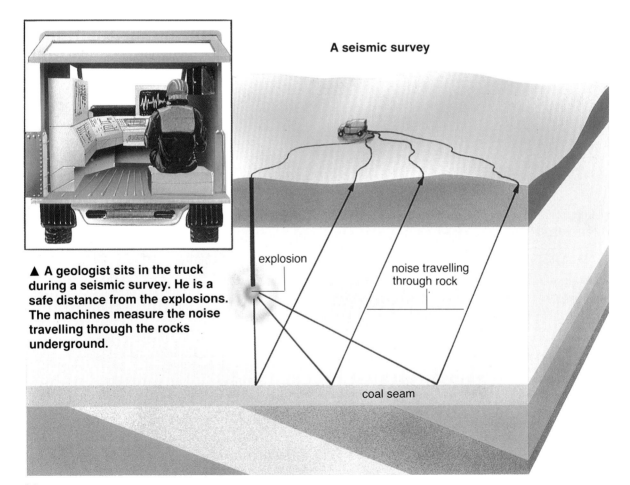

▲ A geologist sits in the truck during a seismic survey. He is a safe distance from the explosions. The machines measure the noise travelling through the rocks underground.

**A seismic survey**

explosion

noise travelling through rock

coal seam

of a coal seam in this core. They can also find out how deep the seam is below the surface.

## Coal under the sea

A lot of the world's coal lies under the sea. It is only the coal near the shore which is mined today. This is because the miners have to make a mine shaft from the coast and tunnel under the sea. The tunnels under the North Sea from Wearmouth coal mine in Britain are over ten kilometres long. Coal taken out of mines like these travels by conveyor belt or underground train. It passes through the undersea tunnels to the mine shaft on land. Then, it is taken up to the surface. The coal can be shipped from a nearby port. Transport by ship is cheaper over longer distances than sending the coal by train or truck. This is because the ship can carry more coal than a train or a truck.

Mining under the sea, or **offshore** mining, has another advantage. It does not cause problems when the seabed sinks after the coal has been removed deep below. This is called **subsidence**. Subsidence often damages buildings standing on the land above a coal mine.

Miners in the future may find new ways of mining coal under the seabed. Special ships are already being used to drill hundreds of metres into the seabed to look for new coal.

▶ At the test site, a geologist takes a sausage-shaped core from the drill rod. More rods are piled up against the drill in the background. The core is pushed out of the drill rod by a jet of water or a special pole. Some samples are sent to the laboratory.

# A deep coal mine

Many coal mines today are more than one kilometre deep. The invention of the steam engine made it possible to sink deeper mine shafts. Steam pumps pumped out water which would have drowned the miners working below. Steam pumps also **ventilated** the mines by forcing fresh air down the shaft. Steam engines worked the **winding gear** which pulled the heavy tubs, or **skips**, of coal to the surface. Today, electric pumps and motors are used.

## The mine

Two mine shafts are dug when a new coal mine is started. The miners sink one shaft to force fresh air down the mine.

Electric fans keep the air moving down below. The other shaft is used to force the used air back to the surface.

The miners tunnel into the coal seams from the mine shaft. They may work on several seams at once, one above the other. Tunnels in the oldest coal mines are several kilometres long because miners dug out the coal near the shafts a long time ago.

Many hundreds of people work in the large mines. Some people work on the surface. They work in the offices, and organize the transportation of the coal away from the mine.

The highest paid workers are the miners who work at the **coal face**. It is hard work getting the coal out of the seams. The miners go down the pit shaft in an electric lift, called a **cage**. The cage takes them quickly to the bottom of the shaft. Underground trains take them from the shaft to the coal face.

◄ This is a tunnel in a coal mine today. It has steel supports to hold up the roof. Pipes carry fresh air to the coal face. Miners travel along the tunnels in special trains.

► Women coal miners work in some mines today. About 2000 women miners work in the United States. They do the same jobs as men and wear the same clothes.

## The miners

The miners usually work in **shifts**. Each shift lasts a certain number of hours. When one shift ends, another begins. The owners of the mine try to take the coal from the mine 24 hours a day.

The miners change into work clothes at the start of each shift. They wear helmets to protect their heads, as well as kneepads, gloves and strong boots with steel toecaps. They also take electric lamps, powered by batteries, which they attach to their helmets. They need this extra light in the darkest parts of the mine away from the well-lighted tunnels.

The miners are hot, tired and dirty at the end of a shift. They have a shower to get rid of all the dirt. They also change their clothes before they go home.

▲ Computers on the surface control the work in many mines. They operate a lot of the machinery. Computers help to make coal mines safer. They can help cut down the number of accidents.

# Wood and coal resources

Many countries sell, or **export**, wood. It is used to make goods in **industry**. The northern countries buy wood from southern countries leaving them with less fuel wood.

Canada and the USSR have the largest pine, or **coniferous**, forests. These softwoods are often used to make paper.

**The world's wood and coal resources**

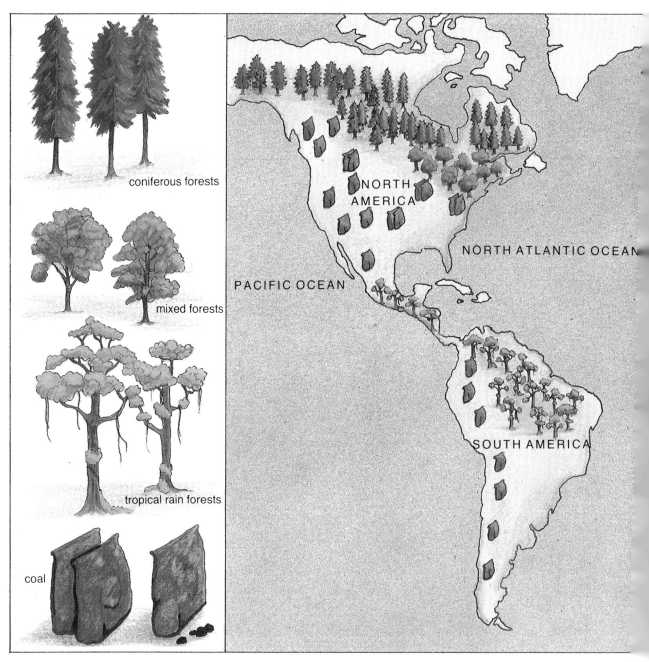

coniferous forests

mixed forests

tropical rain forests

coal

NORTH AMERICA

PACIFIC OCEAN

NORTH ATLANTIC OCEAN

SOUTH AMERICA

Tall leafy trees grow in the **tropical rain forests**. They produce hardwoods, like teak, which are often used to make furniture.

Mixed forests contain many types of tree. The wood is used for making paper and furniture and for building.

The United States, the USSR and China mine most of the world's coal. Some countries export coal to other countries who have no coal. Some people think there may be 7500 million tonnes of coal left in the world. This amount could last about 2500 years.

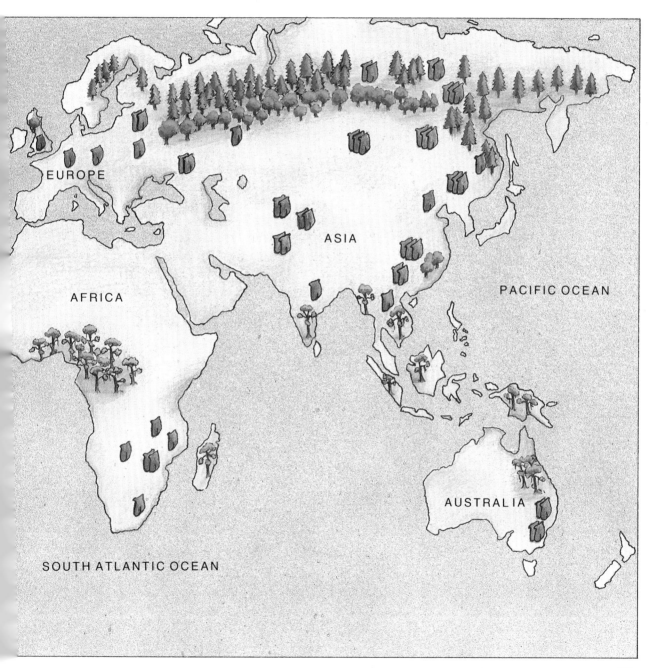

# Cutting the coal

Most mines today use big machines to cut the coal. Conveyor belts are used to take the coal away from the coal face. At the bottom of the shaft, the coal is fed automatically into coal tubs. Then, it is taken to the surface. A coal miner checks that all the machines and processes are working well. The job of a miner is very different from that done by men, women and children over 150 years ago.

## Picks and shovels

Before 1900, most coal was cut by hand with a pick axe. The miners had to crawl along narrow tunnels to get to the coal face. Miners sometimes used gunpowder to bring down the coal, but this was dangerous. They mined coal seams which were often thin, sometimes only 50 cm thick. Many miners spent all day crouched or lying down. Water dripped from the roof of the tunnel. They lay in pools of water. A miner found it hard to cut coal with a pick axe from this position. It was just as hard to shovel coal into a tub.

▲ This miner is cutting coal by hand about 100 years ago. He has no helmet or special clothes to protect him. The coal seam is held up by wooden props.

◄ This miner is working at the coal face in a mine at Longyearbyen on the island of Spitzbergen near the North Pole. He is clearing coal dust made by the coal-cutting machine. You can see why miners need kneepads.

▲ This electric shearer sprays water as it cuts through the coal. The miner on the right controls the shearer with his radio. The steel roof supports are much safer than wooden pit props.

## Machines

The first coal-cutting machines were made in about 1860. American miners used coal-cutting machines long before they were used in the coal mines of Europe. Machines cut most of the coal produced in the United States by 1920. This made American coal much cheaper than coal mined in Europe. Coal-cutting machines were soon used in Germany and Poland. They were not used in Britain until the 1930s.

Large electric cutting machines cut most of the coal today. They slice through coal as if it were butter. Pumps spray water on to the coal face as it is cut. The water keeps clouds of harmful coal dust from flying up in the air. Miners would choke if the pumps spraying water broke down. As the coal cutter rips through the seam, machines automatically put up the steel props to support the roof. Some of these machines are worked by **remote control**.

One machine, the shearer loader, can cut 10 000 tonnes of coal in a day. A single miner with a pick and shovel took 12 500 days, or 34 years, to cut the same amount of coal in 1920.

# Bringing the coal up

Coal is heavy and dirty. It also takes up a lot of space. Today, most coal is put on moving conveyor belts to take it to the mine shaft. Mine cars pulled by trains are also used. The tunnels in many mines slope steeply because they follow the coal seams. Wire ropes have to be used to haul the coal tubs up the steepest slopes.

## Carrying coal in the past

Miners in the early coal mines carried the coal on their backs. Sometimes, they had to climb several ladders to take the coal from where the miners were working to the bottom of the mine shaft. Women and young children carried baskets of coal and dragged heavy coal tubs in many British coal mines 150 years ago.

The women and children wound chains or ropes from the coal tubs around their bodies and between their legs. The chains cut into them and made them bleed. They crouched low to haul these heavy tubs through the narrow tunnels. Small boys and girls, sitting in the dark, opened wooden doors in the tunnels to let them through.

Ponies were used to pull the coal tubs on many underground railways in Britain until about 30 years ago. The best pit ponies were Shetland ponies because they are small and strong. They lived in underground stables and often did not see daylight.

▶ Men, women and children used to carry coal on their backs to the surface.

## Lifting the coal

Buckets and chains were used in the early coal mines to lift the coal up the mine shaft. Women workers wound up buckets of coal when the mines were very shallow. When deeper mines were sunk, the mine owners had to use horses or steam engines to work the winding gear.

Coal today is unloaded from the mine cars or conveyor belts into a container at the foot of the mine shaft. It is fed into skips which take as much as 20 tonnes of coal at one time. The skips are powered by electricity. They take the coal up to the surface.

**A coal mine today**

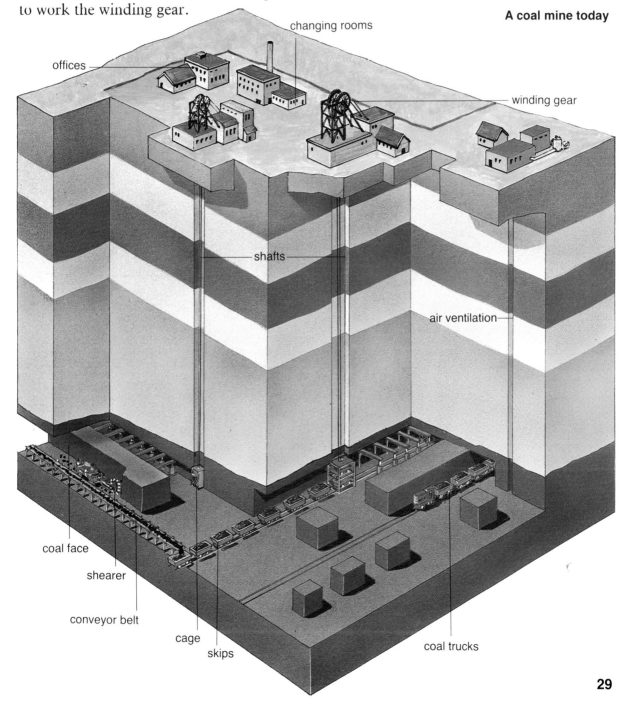

changing rooms

offices

winding gear

shafts

air ventilation

coal face

shearer

conveyor belt

cage

skips

coal trucks

# Using coal fuels

In the early 1700s, coal played a big part in the change from making goods by hand to making goods by machine. There was not much wood available then. Some industries were starting to use coal instead. It was the start of the age of steam.

## Steam power

Steam engines boil water to make steam. They need a fuel which gives off lots of heat. This is why the steam engines which worked the new machines used coal as their fuel, instead of wood. After 1830, more coal was needed when the steam railways were built. Then, 20 years later, ships powered by steam also needed coal. In those days, countries like the United Kingdom and the United States exported coal to countries all over the world. Both countries had rich coalfields. Since then, coal has been found elsewhere. Today, the United States and Australia are among the world's biggest exporters of coal.

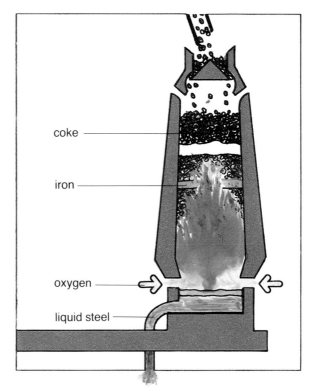

▲ Using coal to make steel.

## Coal at home

Homes in many European and North American towns used coal for heating a hundred years ago. People living in the country still used wood. Fireplaces at that

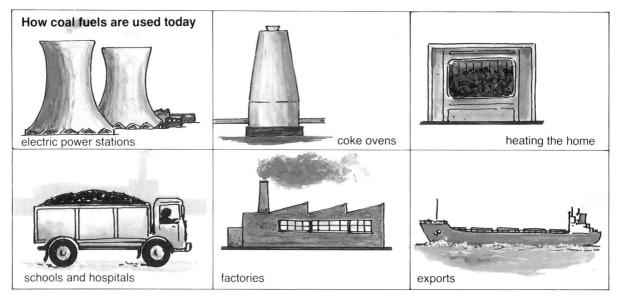

How coal fuels are used today

electric power stations

coke ovens

heating the home

schools and hospitals

factories

exports

time were unable to make good use of the coal. A lot of heat just went up the chimney. Coal fires made the rooms dirty. Chimney smoke made the air outside dirty.

Coal fires and coal stoves used today make far better use of the heat in coal. One type of coal even burns without smoke. This is called smokeless fuel. A few people still use coal for central heating, but most homes today use oil, gas or electricity.

## Industry

**Power stations** which make electricity use most of the coal mined today. Some power stations use as much as 10 000 tonnes of coal a day. The coal heats the water to make steam. The steam is forced through **turbines** to make electricity. A turbine is a wheel with many curved blades. They go around at very high speed. The electric power passes along electric wires to homes and factories. It is much easier to send electricity to a factory than it is to send coal.

Coal is used to make iron into steel. First, the coal has to be changed into **coke**. This is done by baking the coal in an oven without air until it is white hot. Coke produces far more heat than coal because all the gases have been taken out of it. In a steel-making oven, or furnace, the coke burns fiercely. The iron melts in the heat. Oxygen is blown in and most of the carbon in the molten iron is burnt away to make steel. The liquid steel is drawn off from the bottom of the furnace.

▶ Coal is used to melt metals at a foundry in Dunaujváros, Hungary.

# Products from coal

People who burn coal in a stove or fireplace often see colours in the smoke and little jets of flame. Black tar sometimes oozes out of a piece of coal. Gases and substances called **chemicals** in the coal cause these effects. These gases and chemicals are used to make things needed by industry.

▼ A coke and by-products works in England. The coal is brought to the works by train. Then, the by-products made from the coal are used to make goods.

## Coal tar

The chemicals are taken out of the coal by heating it to a high **temperature**. Coal tar is taken from the coal as it is heated. One tonne of coal makes about 35 litres of coal tar. This is a very thick, dark oil. It is heated a second time and mixed with different chemicals to make other products.

Coal tar is used to make explosives, such as TNT. Coal tar is also used to make perfumes, plastics, dyes to colour clothes, and saccharin to sweeten drinks.

## Other products

Coal miners are afraid of finding methane gas when they mine for coal. Methane catches fire quickly. Methane gas was used to light streetlights in the city of

London 180 years ago. Later, people used the gas to light their homes and in their gas cookers. It is not used very much today.

Ways have been found to make petrol from coal. This means that countries without oil can make their own petrol. South Africa, for instance, has lots of cheap coal but it has little oil. Many cars in South Africa now run on petrol made from coal.

## Waste products

The waste products from coal are also useful. Rock waste from coal mining is made into bricks. Other waste is used to fill holes and make banks at the sides of new roads.

▼ The products below are all examples of the variety of goods which can be made from coal.

detergents

fertilizers

explosives

cleaners

road tar

soaps

coal

perfumes

plastics

cosmetics

linoleum

adhesives

paints

nylon

ink

disinfectants

# Coal and gas

Coal fires heat only a few homes today, yet coal is still a useful fuel. Coal is used to make much of the world's electricity. It once was used to make much of the world's coal gas.

## Gaslights

Two hundred years ago, the houses of big cities like New York and London were lit by candles at night. People did not walk on the city streets at night because they were so dark. There were no streetlights.

In 1784, John Clayton collected the coal gas given off when coal was heated. He used the gas to light up his house in Scotland. Then, in 1798, William Murdock

◀ Many city streets used to have gaslights. Lamplighters had to go around and light the lamps each night. Electric street lights now come on automatically.

used coal gas to light a factory in Birmingham, England. He is often said to be the inventor of coal gas.

It was a German, Friedrich Winzer, who first used gas for street lighting. In 1807, he showed people in London that coal gas could be used to light the streets. He built a big **gasworks** in London in 1812. In the following year he laid pipes from his gasworks, to light the streets in a part of the city called Westminster.

**Making gas from coal**

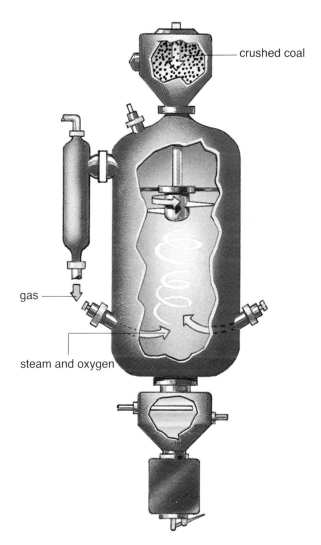

crushed coal

gas

steam and oxygen

▲ Gasholders rise as they fill with gas. This one is very full. The coal on the right will be used to make more gas.

## Gas from coal

To get gas from coal, bituminous coal was heated to a high temperature inside an oven. The coal gas was made as the hot coal turned into coke. The gas was collected in pipes and stored in large round containers called gas holders.

Gasworks today make coal gas in a different way. It is called the Lurgi Process. First, the coal is crushed. Then, it is mixed with steam and oxygen. This makes the gas. It is a better way of making gas because it makes more gas and leaves less coke.

Today, natural gas provides much of the gas used in the world for cooking and heating. Natural gas gives twice as much heat as coal gas. It is also cheaper. Natural gas is sometimes found under the earth by people looking for oil. It is a fossil fuel like coal. One day, there will be none left.

The Lurgi Process can be used to make natural gas as well as coal gas. The gas it produces is called substitute natural gas, or **SNG** for short.

# The air around us

The air around us is called the **atmosphere**. It is like a thick blanket. It stretches all the way around the surface of the world. We cannot see the atmosphere, but we know it is there. It has several layers. The air we breathe is in the lowest layer. Air is made up of different gases. Most of the gas is nitrogen. It is mixed with some oxygen. Oxygen is the gas we use when we breathe.

## A protective layer

Millions of years ago, there was very little oxygen in the atmosphere. This changed when the first plants began to grow. They made oxygen. The new oxygen in the air made it possible for creatures to live and breathe. The plants made so much oxygen that a thin layer of **ozone** began to form in the atmosphere about 30 km above the Earth's surface. Ozone is a gas formed from oxygen. The layer of ozone keeps the Earth from getting too much heat from the Sun.

nitrogen

oxygen

other gases

**Gases in the air**

# Clean air

We must keep the atmosphere clean because it gives life to all living things. This is why many people are worried by the problem of air **pollution**. Air pollution causes illnesses, such as bronchitis. It even makes stone carvings crumble away. It can also kill the trees which help to make the oxygen we need to live and breathe.

▼ Trees and plants need sunlight to turn carbon dioxide in the air into carbon and oxygen. The trees and plants use the carbon to make their food. They release the unwanted oxygen. People and animals live by breathing oxygen from the air.

Wood burnt on fires and coal burnt in power stations adds extra carbon dioxide to the air. Fumes from traffic exhausts adds nitrogen to the air. At the same time, we are chopping down large areas of trees on Earth. We need the trees to help us keep the right balance in the air around us.

# Spoiling the air

All living creatures depend on the atmosphere. It changed once when plants began to grow and make oxygen. Some experts say it is changing again because people have been burning wood and coal for hundreds of years.

## Smoke and fumes

Smoke and fumes released into the air cause air pollution. We know that smoke can harm the air we breathe. Thick smoke from British chimneys once mixed with fog to form a choking yellow air called **smog**. This smog killed 4000 people in Britain in 1952. The smog affected those people who had problems when they breathed. Air pollution also caused the deaths of about 400 people in New York City in 1962.

Cities, like Pittsburgh in the United States and Glasgow in Scotland, once had a constant cloud of smoke above them. This is why the British and American governments passed Clean Air Acts in 1956 (UK) and 1970 (USA) to lower the amount of smoke and fumes released into the air.

▼ Smoke pours from the chimneys of a small factory in Beijing, China. Most Chinese factories use coal.

Although the sky is clearer, pollution of the atmosphere still continues. Many power stations burn coal to make electricity. Coal contains a substance called **sulphur**. When sulphur burns, it makes a gas called sulphur dioxide. You cannot see this gas, but it harms people if they breathe it into their lungs. This is why power stations are built with very tall chimneys. The chimneys send the harmful fumes high into the air. The fumes are carried away from people's houses by the wind. Sometimes the wind carries the fumes to other countries.

▼ **The greenhouse effect traps the Earth's heat.**

## Wastes and the weather

The amount of carbon dioxide in the upper atmosphere has grown with the burning of wood and coal. By the year 2050, there may be twice as much carbon dioxide in the air as there was in 1850. The carbon dioxide in the air may keep heat from leaving the Earth's atmosphere. It would trap the Earth's heat like the air inside a greenhouse. People think it will cause the weather, or **climate**, to change in many parts of the world. This would cause drought in one place and high rainfall and floods in another. It would also affect the amount of food grown in different parts of the world.

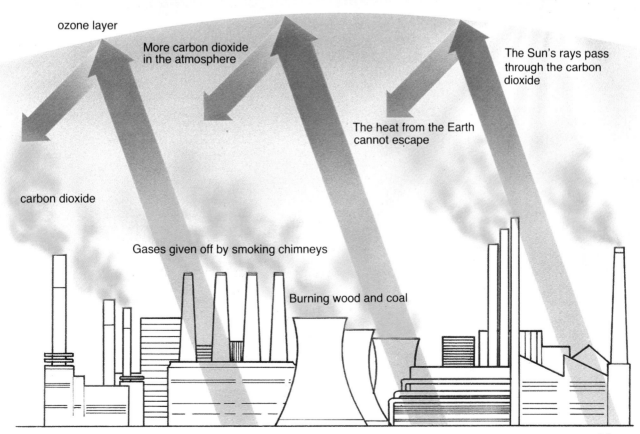

ozone layer

More carbon dioxide in the atmosphere

The Sun's rays pass through the carbon dioxide

The heat from the Earth cannot escape

carbon dioxide

Gases given off by smoking chimneys

Burning wood and coal

# Forests at risk

The size of the world's forests is getting smaller. Each year, forests covering an area about as big as Britain are chopped down. This is called deforestation. It affects the plants and animals in the forests. They have fewer places to grow and live. Deforestation affects us, too. Each year, less oxygen is made because there are fewer trees. This is why it is important that new trees are planted to take the place of those cut down or those which die. It takes time for trees to grow, but planting forests will bring other benefits as well. Planting new forests will create more jobs and provide more timber for the world in 20 years time.

## Cutting down trees

Most of the trees being cut down are in the hot rain forests of Brazil, Central Africa and South East Asia. People clear the forests to make way for land on which they can grow crops to sell, such as fruit and sugar. They build houses for the workers employed in the new mines being opened in the forest lands. They clear trees so that roads can be built. They cut down timber to be sold to countries with little wood of their own.

Many of the people who live in the forests do not see why they should plant new trees to take the place of those they cut down. They want to use the land for their new homes and farms.

## Harmful rain

The problem of deforestation also affects the coniferous forests of the north. Many trees in Europe and North America are dying. The reasons why they are dying are not known for certain. Some people think it is because the smoke and fumes from power stations and from car exhausts are spoiling the atmosphere. They say that when rain falls through this polluted air, it picks up harmful chemicals which turn it into **acid rain**. The acid rain falls many kilometres away from where the smoke and fumes went into the atmosphere. Acid rain may have killed many of the trees in the Black Forest in Germany and in forests in North America. It may also have poisoned lakes in Norway and Sweden, so that fish no longer live there.

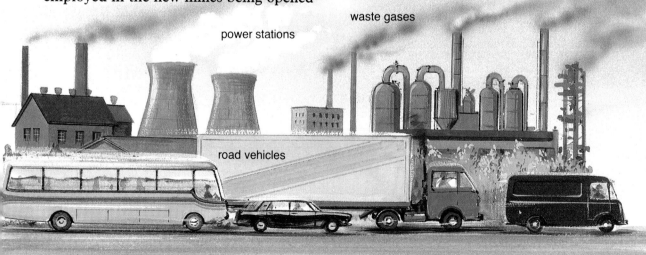

waste gases

power stations

road vehicles

◀ Trees are cut down for food so that farmers can grow crops. Plants and animals die out when their forest homes disappear.

▶ We should use less wood and not waste energy. Other sources of energy should be used if possible.

◀ People have to walk a long way to collect wood. They burn manure instead of spreading it on the land.

▶ Acid rain damages the needles on pine trees. The rain sinks into the ground, too. It kills the trees' roots.

◀ Soil is washed away for good because there are no trees to hold the forest land together any more.

◀ Forest experts are needed to help people replant trees near their homes. Trees can be treated like a farm crop. Dead branches provide wood without cutting down the whole tree.

chemicals returning to the Earth as acid rain

chemicals blown by the wind

**Acid rain falls on areas a long way from the smoking chimneys.**

# Guarding our fuel supplies

We must make better use of the energy supplies we have. Otherwise, the people of the future may find it hard to live on Earth.

## Burning fossil fuels

When we burn fossil fuels, we are burning fuels that cannot be replaced. Coal, oil and natural gas are non-renewable sources of energy. There is only a limited supply. They will all disappear in time.

The world's supplies of oil and natural gas will have gone in about a hundred years time if they continue to be burned at the same rate as today. People will have to use more coal in the future. There is still enough coal left in the world to last many hundreds of years, if it is used wisely.

## Saving energy

One way of saving the world's fuel supplies is to try to make them last longer. This can be done by not wasting energy. Wasted energy can be seen in every town. Hot water is poured down drains, which wastes heat. Heat goes up a chimney to heat the sky instead of the home. Heat warms empty rooms.

People can do something to save energy. A home owner can keep more heat inside the home by installing double glazed windows. A thick layer of insulation laid on the floor in the roof space stops heat from escaping into the sky. A shower uses less hot water than a bath. It does not take as much energy to heat the water.

Many of the machines we use can save energy as well. Some cars use less petrol

▼ This forest in Malaysia was burned down. The new plants will take many years to grow into trees. Pine trees grow the most quickly. They can be used in 15 to 20 years. Hardwoods, like teak, take much longer.

than others. We can walk or ride bikes instead of going by car. A bicyclist's energy comes from food which can be replaced instead of from fossil fuels which cannot.

## New types of energy

In the future, we can make more use of the Sun to heat our homes. **Solar panels** on the roofs can take heat from the Sun and use it to heat water. Other new sources of energy are already in use. The most promising are those we know we can always use again, such as the wind, water and the Sun itself. Windmills make electricity. Hydro-electric power stations use water power.

▶ We cannot replace the coal taken from under the ground. Coal is a non-renewable fuel. We can replace the farmland on the surface. Many old mines are now farms or parks. The opencast mine on the right closed when all the coal had been taken out. The picture below shows the same land which is now used as a park.

# Looking ahead

There is no shortage of coal in the world at the present time. New coal mines are opened every year. The first coal mines only lasted a year or so. Today, most of the new coal mines will produce coal for about 75 years until they are closed.

The real problem is what to do with the coal. We can burn it to make electricity or gas. We can also use it as a source of such products as coal tar and plastics. We can even leave it in the ground for the use of the people still to be born.

## The future for coal

We can guess at some of the things that may happen to coal in the future. Better ways of using coal to make heat may be found. Safer ways of getting coal out of the ground may be found. **Robot** miners controlled by computers could well be used in future coal mines. Ways of mining the thick seams of coal under the seabed will also be found. The coal mines of the future may be in the middle of the sea instead of on land.

## The use of energy

Some people use far more of the world's energy than others. On average, people in the United States use up to ten times as much energy as the people who live in most South American countries. One person in every six in the world lives in India, yet the Indians use only one-fifth of the world's energy.

The people of the world who use the most energy live in Europe, North America, the USSR, Japan and Australia. They have about a quarter of the world's people but use about three-quarters of the world's supplies of energy. The world must find ways of making new energy available to all the peoples of the world, not just to those who live in these countries.

The Sun will still be shining a billion years from now. The Sun gave us most of the energy we use today. We can only hope that a safe way will be found of using the Sun's heat and light to provide all the energy the world will need in the future.

**Coal mining under the sea**

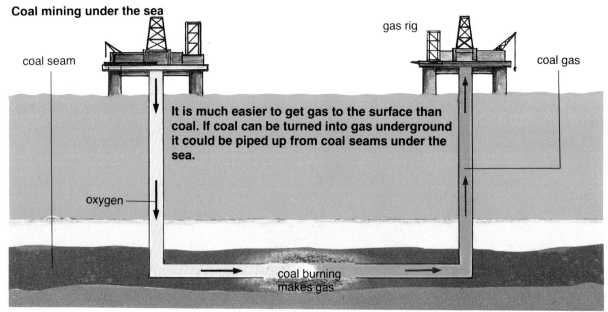

coal seam

gas rig

coal gas

It is much easier to get gas to the surface than coal. If coal can be turned into gas underground it could be piped up from coal seams under the sea.

oxygen

coal burning makes gas

Wood and coal cannot supply all the energy the world needs. Two-thirds of the world is covered by the sea. The energy of the Sun and the sea will always be there. We have to find out how to use it.

# Glossary

**acid rain:** rain which poisons trees and plants as it falls on them. Acid rain contains poisons from factories, coal-burning power stations and car exhaust fumes which were in the air

**adit mine:** a mine tunnelled into the side of a hill

**anthracite:** a hard, shiny black coal containing 94% carbon and 3% oxygen. It burns very slowly and makes no smoke

**atmosphere:** the mixture of gases that surround a planet. The Earth's atmosphere is the air

**bell pit:** a shallow coal mine shaped like a bell

**bituminous coal:** a soft black coal containing about 85% carbon. It is used for house coal and for making coal tar and coal gas

**borehole:** a hole drilled in the ground in order to look for minerals like coal and oil

**cage:** a lift which takes miners up and down a mine shaft

**calories:** a measurement of energy in the form of heat. Burning coal gives off energy as heat. Food is eaten to give animals energy. The heat or energy in a piece of coal or a potato is measured in calories

**cannel coal:** a dull, black hard coal which burns steadily with a flame like a candle

**carbon:** an important substance found in fuels, foods and all living things

**carbon dioxide:** a gas found in the air. All animals breathe out carbon dioxide. Plants use carbon dioxide to make food

**Carboniferous period:** a stage in the history of the Earth which began about 300 million years ago. The name means 'carbon bearing' because many of the rocks made at this time contain coal which is made of carbon

**charcoal:** wood that has been partly burned over several days and then cooled. When it is burned again, it makes more heat than ordinary wood

**chemical:** any substance which can change when joined or mixed with another substance

**chlorophyll:** the substance which makes leaves green. Plants use chlorophyll to make their own food

**climate:** the weather of an area or a country through the year. Climate differs from one area to another. Deserts have hot dry climates. Mountain tops have cold climates

**coal face:** the part of the coal seam that is being cut by miners

**coke:** a fuel made by baking coal in an oven to take out the gas. Coke is mostly carbon and gives off much more heat than untreated coal

**coniferous:** describes trees that keep their seeds in cones. Most coniferous trees are evergreen like pine, spruce and fir trees

**conveyor belt:** a very long strip or belt of strong material which is moved over rollers by a motor. Things put on the flat surface are carried along

**deforestation:** the cutting down of all the trees over a large area. Chopping down whole forests

**drift mine:** an underground coal mine reached by a long sloping tunnel or drift from the surface

**electricity:** a type of energy or power which can travel along wires. It is used to heat and light homes, run factories and work many machines

**energy cycle:** the change from heat or work energy to stored energy and from stored energy back to heat or work energy

**export:** to send goods to another country to be sold

**fossil:** the remains of animals and plants which lived millions of years ago

**fossil fuels:** material which can be burned that comes from the remains of animals and plants which lived millions of years ago. Coal and oil are fossil fuels

**fuel:** material which burns. Fuel burned in engines makes power for movement

**gasworks:** a place where gas is made by burning fuel and collecting the gas that is given off

**geologist:** a scientist who studies rocks and the history of the Earth

**hydrogen:** a gas which is very light and burns easily

**industry:** the work to do with the making or producing of goods, often in a factory

**lignite:** brown coal. It crumbles easily and looks like wood. It has less carbon and more oxygen than black coal and does not give off as much heat

**longwall:** a way of mining in which coal is taken from along the length or long wall of a coal seam

**methane gas:** a gas made by rotting vegetation. It is found in coal seams and marshland

**non-renewable:** something which cannot be replaced or renewed when it is used up

**offshore:** at a distance from the shore

**opencast mining:** a way of mining coal which lies near the surface. The coal is dug out from above

**overburden:** the rock and earth above a coal seam which has to be removed in order to dig out or quarry coal which lies near the surface

**oxygen:** the gas found in the air and water. Oxygen is very important to all plants and animals. We cannot breathe without oxygen

**ozone:** a gas made from oxygen. It helps protect the Earth from the strong rays of the Sun

**peat:** partly rotted plants in wet marshland. Peat is soft and spongy to touch, but it can be dried out and used as a fuel

**pollution:** something which dirties or poisons the air, land or water, such as waste chemicals from factories

**population:** the total number of people living in a country or in one place

**power station:** a large building where electricity is made

**pressure:** the action of one thing pressing on or against something else

**prop:** a support, used to hold something up. Strong props are used to hold up the roof of a tunnel

**remote control:** the control of something from a distance, usually through radio or electric signals

**renewable:** something which can be replaced or put back after being used

**robot:** a machine that can perform jobs automatically. Robots are usually controlled by a computer

**room and pillar:** a way of mining in which a large amount of the coal in an area is left standing as thick pillars to support the roof. The coal was cut around the pillar to make a large room

**safety lamp:** a lamp used in mining. Gauze surrounds the lamp to keep the flame inside from setting fire to explosive gases

**seam:** a layer of coal

**sediment:** solid matter that settles to the bottom of a liquid. Sand and silt will fall to the bed of the sea or a river

**sedimentary rock:** a type of rock which was formed from sediments. These include sandstones from sand, clays from mud, and limestones from the shells of sea creatures

**seismic survey:** a way of finding out about rocks below the Earth's surface by setting off a series of controlled explosions. Instruments measure the speed of the shock waves from these explosions through the ground

**shaft:** a deep hole in the ground

**shift:** a working period of several hours. Jobs in a factory, coal mine, or hospital are often divided into shifts so that the work can go on all day and all night without stopping

**skip:** a strong open container used for carrying heavy materials. This is the huge bucket which lifts coal to the top of a mine shaft

**smog:** a poisonous combination of smoke and fog

**SNG:** Substitute Natural Gas made by forcing steam and oxygen through powdered coal. This is called the Lurgi Process

**solar panel:** a large flat area, or panel, that contains many solar cells. Each solar cell collects energy from the Sun's rays and turns it into electricity. Simple solar panels can be used to heat water

**stove:** a cooker or heater which can be enclosed on all sides to keep in the heat

**strip mining:** a way of mining coal which lies near the surface. The coal is dug out from above

**subsidence:** sinking down. In areas that have been heavily mined, the ground sometimes drops into the holes that are left

**sulphur:** a yellow substance found in the Earth. When it burns it has a blue flame and gives off a strong smell. It is used in many industries

**temperature:** the measurement of the heat or coldness of something. Temperature is measured in degrees

**topsoil:** the rich soil on the surface in which crops grow

**tropical rain forest:** a very hot, damp forest found in the regions close to the Equator. Tropical forests have tall trees and plants which grow very close together

**turbine:** a wheel which has many curved blades. It is turned by water or gas. Turbines drive machines which make electricity

**ventilation:** a system for bringing fresh air into a room or building

**winding gear:** the machinery for raising and lowering a lift, especially in a mine shaft

**work:** in science, any movement, effort or action which involves the movement of energy from one area to another

# Index